# SQUASH

# PLAY·THE·GAME

# SQUASH

Dick Hawkey ·

Ward Lock Limited · London

First published in Great Britain in 1988
by Ward Lock Limited, 8 Clifford Street
London W1X 1RB, an Egmont Company

Reprinted 1988

Series Editor Ian Morrison
Designed by Anita Ruddell
Illustrations by Bob Williams

Text set in Helvetica
by Hourds Typographica, Stafford, England
Printed and bound in Great Britain
by Richard Clay Ltd, Bungay, Suffolk

**British Library Cataloguing in Publication Data**
Hawkey, Dick
Play the game : Squash
    1. Squash rackets (Game)
    I. Title    II. Series
    796.34'3        GV1004

    ISBN 0-7063-6662-X

# *Acknowledgments*

The author and publishers would like to
thank Colorsport for supplying the
photographs reproduced in this book.

*Frontispiece:* **Jahangir Khan, one of the
greatest players of recent years, about to
pounce on the backhand.**

# CONTENTS

# FOREWORD

It was with great pleasure that I accepted the publisher's invitation to write a foreword to *Play the Game: Squash*. I have been playing squash for many years now, and not once has the magic of this great game worn off. I can remember what it was like to begin playing squash, and I welcome the publication of this bright new book, telling the novice player all he or she needs to know.

The section on the history and development of squash provides an interesting and useful background to all the practical information and advice which follows. Some beginners find the 'language' of squash a little difficult to follow at first, but the 'Terminology' section clearly explains the most awkward of expressions. There is a lot of useful information about equipment too, which will help anyone bewildered by their first trip to the squash court!

The real strength of this new book lies in the innovative 'Game Guide' and 'Rules Clinic' sections. All the essential rules are clearly explained, and many of the problems which beginners often experience are carefully analysed and sorted out.

The 'Technique' section of the book does not blind the beginner with science, but instead explains the basic shots as far as is necessary. There are lots of helpful drawings and diagrams to get the various points across.

As squash is becoming an increasingly popular spectator sport, it is nice to see some emphasis on the visual side of the game, with photographs of leading players in action and facts about important innovations like the 'goldfish bowl' court and the 'Teleball'.

# FOREWORD

*Play the Game: Squash* is altogether an extremely useful book, and I welcome it wholeheartedly as a valuable guide and incentive to all players and spectators of my sport. I sincerely hope that people of all ages will follow its lead and get as much enjoyment out of squash as I have done during my career.

**Jahangir Khan**

# HISTORY & DEVELOPMENT OF SQUASH

In the beginning there was rackets – a game with a long history, played in a huge barn of a court with a hard ball, and with rackets which were stronger versions of today's squash racket. It is clear that rackets was the parent of squash since most of the rules, the court markings and the jargon are the same.

One theory is that squash developed around 150 years ago at Harrow School, where boys awaiting their game of rackets knocked a ball around in an open area with three walls outside the actual court. Eventually they were requested to refrain from this practice, perhaps because of noise, or broken windows. If you must play, it was insisted, use a soft or 'squash' type of ball. Clearly the boys found that they could do things with this ball that they could not do with the hard rackets ball. Some boys apparently became so attracted to this new game that they continued to play it in suitable outhouses or other areas at home, and it became popular enough at around the turn of the century for the Bath Club in London to install courts for the new game of 'squash rackets'.

However, as early as 1874 in a coaching manual for racket sports there is a brief reference to squash in the rackets section, so clearly the game was becoming popular at that time.

An alternative theory is that the game sprang to life in the Fleet Prison, from where prisoners were transported to Australia. I have heard the great Jonah Barrington remark that this would explain the interest shown by Australians in squash! I prefer the Harrow theory, and certainly there are still quite a number of rather odd courts with peculiar dimensions dotted around the country, suggesting that at some stage families built their own courts.

By the First World War, a number of London social clubs had built courts, all based on the dimensions of the original courts at the Bath Club and Lord's. Those dimensions have remained in use to the present day. However, even though the dimensions were constant, location and construction varied tremendously; some, like

**Hashim Khan, perhaps the greatest player of all time, still at it in his vintage years. He was renowned for his electrifying speed.**

the RAC and Lansdowne, were in the same area as a heated swimming pool, making them uncomfortably hot, whilst the 'outside walled' courts at Lord's, Queens and Hurlingham brought instant risk of pneumonia. Ceiling heights and wall materials also varied a great deal, and for a long time, individual clubs used different balls, and indeed the one dimension that was not standard was the height of the 'tin' at the bottom of the front wall.

It is unfortunate that before the game became standardized here, it had found its way to America. The pioneers there developed a different form of the game, played with a hard ball on a narrower court. The difference between the international soft-ball game and the American hard-ball version is that the former has two players chasing a small black ball round the court, while the latter has a small black ball chasing two players round the court!

Originally the game was played purely for fun, but shortly after the First World War the major championships, the home internationals and league squash began. In 1929 the Squash Rackets Association was formed and became the governing body of the game, not only in England but throughout the squash playing world. One of its first actions was to institute the Open Championship. To begin the championship one of the day's great players, Charles Read, was nominated and then challenged and beaten by another English professional, Don Butcher. It was the Egyptians however who dominated the Open, with Amr Bey before World War II and with Mahmoud Karim after it.

In 1950 the first of the great Pakistanis appeared – Hashim Khan, followed by his brother Azam and then cousin Roshan, who is the father of Jahangir, the world number one for most of the 1980s. In between the years of Khan domination, the British player Jonah Barrington won the title six times, and Geoff Hunt from Australia eight.

In 1969, the Squash Rackets Association ceased to be the governing body of the game following the formation of the International Squash Rackets Federation. Originally there were seven founder members, England, Australia, New Zealand, Pakistan, South Africa, India and Egypt, but many other countries have since joined as full or associate members.

The game was completely revolutionized by the invention of the glass back wall, which allowed many more spectators to view the matches, so increasing the income of host clubs and associations. The single glass wall then developed into the portable all-see-through court – hereinafter called the 'goldfish bowl' – allowing as many as 3,000 spectators to view major events, and allowing the game to be televised. In turn this has meant a great increase in sponsorship, and therefore in prize money.

The results of these innovations have been in the main very beneficial to the game, but it has to be admitted that the increased rewards for winning have also led to a different attitude among the players compared to the days when squash was played for fun or for a pint of beer, and the rules have had to be tightened up to cope with this new ruthlessness.

The Squash Rackets Association, still the governing body in England, has done a great deal over the years to assist in the development of the game, in the training of coaches and referees and in the building and maintenance of courts. Most countries in which squash is played have their own associations.

In addition to the great advances at the top competitive level, there has also been a vast increase in the number of players at club and school level. There are very few places in this country where there is not a squash club or a leisure centre of some sort with courts. Despite all I have said about spectators, the attraction of squash remains in the playing of the game. Clubs nowadays often run several teams in the local leagues and also have various internal ladders, leagues and knockout competitions. Most clubs either have their own professional or coach, so anyone wishing to take up the game will have no difficulty in obtaining guidance. Anyone wishing to know where their nearest club is should contact the SRA.

Another major factor in the squash boom is that in recent years there has been a great increase in the desire to be fit and healthy, as well as an increase in the amount of leisure time available to the average person. Many people find squash ideal for keeping fit; not only is it much more fun to hit a ball round a court than to jog up and down streets, but with squash, one is not limited by the weather. There are now thought to be some three million players in this country.

There has also been tremendous growth in junior squash with tournaments, county and national squad coaching etc., for the Under 12s and even below. In addition the Veterans (over 45) are more numerous than ever, and the Vintage championships (over 55) are hard fought and very skilful affairs, with some excellent squash being played.

All this means that anyone, of whatever age, who wishes to take up squash is able to do so, and will very quickly find his or her own level, but with every opportunity to improve and progress up the ladder. All games have become more expensive over the years, and squash is no exception, but it is certainly cheaper than many games. Squash needs only one ball and a racket. One can always avoid a club subscription by hiring a court, but the fun that one can have in a club, and the opportunities for coaching and competition, are well worth a few pounds. So – anyone for squash? Come and join us!

# EQUIPMENT & TERMINOLOGY

**S**quash is a court game and is played in a squash court. The court itself is a four-walled room, 9·75m × 6·4m (32ft × 21ft). It is similar to lawn tennis in many ways, except that a wall has been built in place of the tennis net, and instead of a rally being played over the net to the opponent on the other side, the ball now rebounds from the wall to the opponent in the same playing area. There are also walls

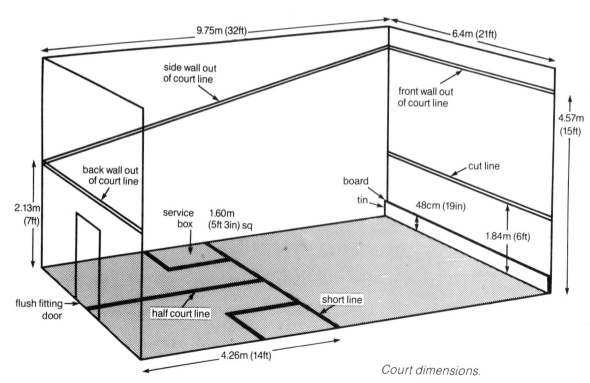

*Court dimensions.*

*Shake hands with the racket.*

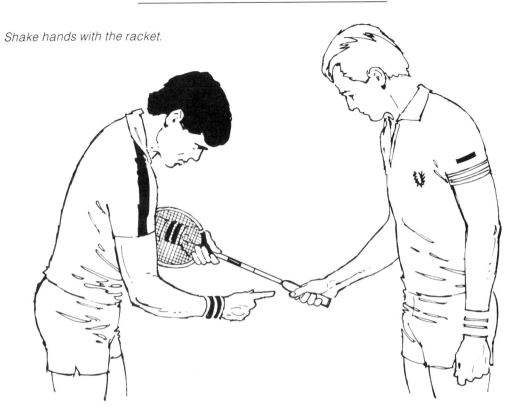

down the 'tramlines' and across the baseline, so to speak, and provided the ball hits the 'front' wall above the 'tin' – the squash equivalent of the net – it can rebound off any of the other walls on its way to or from the front wall. The other walls are the side walls and the back wall, and they continue to be so named even when they are made of glass or plastic.

The only equipment one needs is a racket, plus of course a ball. Rackets now come in a wide range of styles and prices. The top players use rackets of graphite construction which are very expensive and certainly unnecessary for a beginner. For years, rackets made of any material other than wood were illegal, for safety reasons. However, after many experiments and tests, various other materials were deemed acceptable, including certain types of metal rackets. The advantage of the new rackets appears to be that they provide a larger area off which the ball will rebound well. With wooden rackets it is necessary to hit the ball in its centre to achieve maximum force, while the areas towards the frame are rather dead. However, wooden rackets are perfectly satisfactory for beginners, and can be bought for only a few pounds.

When choosing a racket, a player will find considerable differences in weight, balance and grip. The overall weights vary, and even in rackets of the same weight, the 'feel' will be different according to the 'point of balance', i.e., some rackets feel heavier if the weight is in the head, others lighter if it is in the handle. It is largely a matter of finding which type suits you over a period of time. Grips too vary a great deal, both in shape and material. Players who find that their hands sweat a great deal may be well advised to use a towelling grip, which can be replaced easily when it becomes worn; others may prefer a leather grip, or one of the rubber-based materials. Obviously a good and comfortable grip is essential, and it is highly dangerous if the racket is likely to fly across the court and fell your opponent.

There are no particular weights or shapes of racket that are better than others; all that matters is that it feels right to its owner and he has confidence in it. Perhaps the best way of choosing a racket is to hold it in front of you with the non-racket hand, handle towards you and head vertical, and then 'shake hands' with it with the racket hand. The one that feels comfortable and appears to allow you to play forehand and backhand strokes with no change of grip, is probably the right one for you.

Balls come in basically four different speeds – I say basically because in the major championships, players use a 'double yellow dot' or in matches in the 'goldfish bowl' which are being televised, a special 'Teleball' is used which is designed to show up clearly on television. Ordinary players use balls marked with coloured dots – blue, red, white or yellow.

In order to enjoy a game of squash, it must be possible to have reasonable rallies. The colours indicate the speed of the ball concerned, blue being the fastest and yellow the slowest. A ball is faster in a hot court than a cold one, and gains in speed the more and the harder it is hit. Thus, two schoolgirl beginners on a cold court would need a blue dot to have any chance of a rally, but two competent club players would

*This is a comfortable grip for both forehand and backhand.*

find a blue dot bounding all over the court, and whatever shots they played, there would be no way of ending the rally.

Players must therefore select the sensible ball for their own standard and one suitable for the temperature in the court in which they are going to play. Most matches are played with yellow dots, but in extreme wintry conditions in cold courts with outside walls, it may be sensible to use the slightly faster white dots. The actual fabric of the ball itself (rubber), may be black or green, and some clubs insist that only green balls are used in the belief that these will not cause the walls to be marked to the same extent.

As far as clothing is concerned, it is desirable to wear white clothing or at least matching pastel attire – this is to present an acceptable background against which the opponent can sight the ball. The one essential is that shoes are not black-soled and will not mark the floor.

**The teleball: designed purely for use in front of the television cameras, it can be re-touched to restore its visibility. Each teleball costs about £100.**

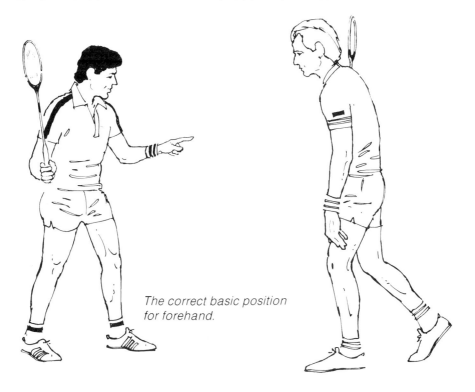

*The correct basic position for forehand.*

# TERMINOLOGY

## Court markings

First of all, it should be pointed out that if a ball hits a line in squash it is always 'out' whereas in tennis a ball hitting a line is 'good'. Similarly, there is no squash equivalent to the net-cord shot in tennis when the ball hits the top of the net and remains in play. Once a ball in squash has touched the red board at the top of the 'tin', the rally is over and the player responsible for that shot has lost it.

***Out of court line***   This is the line going round all four walls marking the upper limit of the play area. A ball is 'out', and so loses the rally, if it strikes the line or any part of the wall above it, or any part of the roof or anything hanging from it (lights, etc.), or goes over any beam or rafter. A ball may go higher than the beam, etc., elsewhere in the roof area but must not go over it. The line is 4·57m (15ft) above the floor on the front wall, and 2·13m (7ft) high on the back wall, and the sloping lines down the side walls join these two lines.

***Tin and board***   Across the bottom of the front wall there is the 'tin', normally topped by a red-painted board, the top of which is 0·48m (19in) from the floor. This is the equivalent to the net in tennis and any ball not clearing this loses the rally. The tin should be fixed so that it makes a loud, unmistakable noise when struck by the ball. All the other lines refer only to the service. These are:

***Cut line***   This is the line across the front wall at a height of 1·83m (6ft). A good service has to hit the front wall between the cut line and the out of court line.

***Short line***   This is the line that goes across the floor parallel to the front and rear wall, 4·26m (13ft 10in) from the latter.

***Half court line***   This is the line that runs parallel with the side walls from the centre of the short line to the rear wall. A correct service has to rebound from the front wall and land in the opposite rear 'quarter' of the court formed by the short and half court lines.

***Service boxes***   Just to the rear of the short line by either side wall are two squares 1·60m (5ft 3in) long and wide, which indicate the area in which the server must have at least one foot when he actually strikes the ball.

***The T***   So called, for obvious reasons, is the spot where the short and half court lines join in the centre of the court. This is the position players aim to reach after each shot in order to 'dominate' the court and to get to any stroke their opponent may play. All lines shall be 50mm (2in) in width, and coloured red.

## The officials

At most championship matches, there are two officials, the 'marker' and the referee. The marker calls the score, makes all the initial decisions about whether the service and the various shots in the rally are good and in general is 'the voice' that keeps the game flowing. However, the referee is in overall charge, and all the marker's calls can be appealed against. The referee decides all appeals and is there to ensure that the match reaches its fair conclusion, which can only be achieved if each rally is fairly decided. He makes all decisions concerning the granting or refusal of lets and the awarding of penalties for obstruction, etc. His decisions are final. In the average club league game there will be only one official normally, and he has to carry out the duties of both the marker and the referee. This is not nearly as onerous as it might sound, and can actually be a very enjoyable task to undertake once a player is experienced and properly acquainted with the requirements of this dual role.

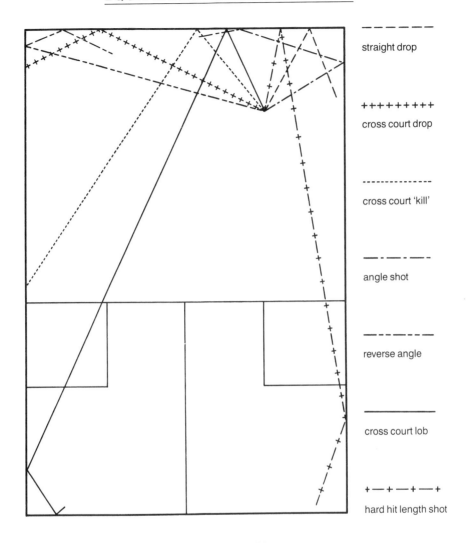

straight drop

++++++++
cross court drop

cross court 'kill'

angle shot

reverse angle

cross court lob

hard hit length shot

*The eight possible shots from a given position.*
*Lob down side wall = same path as hard hit length shot.*

## The strokes

The aim of the game is to hit the ball to the most difficult part of the court for your opponent to reply to, to deceive and wrongfoot him and to work towards the moment when the ball can be finally put beyond his reach. Apart from the service, which will be discussed later, the following shots are used during a rally.

***The drive*** A hard-hit shot, either down the nearest wall or across court, with the aim of forcing your opponent to play his next shot from an awkward position in one of the rear corners of the court.

***The drop*** A gently struck ball, played as close as safety allows to the top of the board, and aimed to drop into the nick

between the side wall and the floor. A straight drop is aimed towards the side wall nearest the player and a cross-court drop is played towards the side wall furthest from him.

**The lob** This is a shot that is hit upwards on to the front wall with the aim of going over the reach of your opponent in the centre of the court, and forcing him to retrieve from a back corner. It can be played down the nearest side wall, but is more effective across court, when the opposite side wall will take more speed off an already 'slow' shot and will make the retrieving process more difficult, since the ball will be more likely to 'die' in the corner.

**The angle or boast** Angles are shots that reach the front wall after striking one of the other walls first. Normally it will be one of the side walls, but players quite frequently find that the only way to return a ball that has gone past them is to hit it upwards against the rear wall and hope it will carry to the front wall; this is known as the 'back wall boast'. Sometimes a ball can only be retrieved by hitting it upwards on to the side wall near the back of the court. Usually, however, angles are attacking shots aimed at deceiving and wrong-footing your opponent.

For example, if you have been consistently hitting drives down your forehand side wall, your opponent may have begun to anticipate this and will be out of position if an angle shot to the forehand wall is played from where it will rebound towards the front backhand corner, diametrically opposite to where he is heading. Angles normally refer to strokes played towards the nearest side wall, and balls pulled across court to the further

**Previous pages: The 'goldfish bowl': looking through the front left-hand corner of the court. The see-through walls have revolutionized squash for the spectator.**

wall are called reverse angles.

The words volley and half volley mean exactly the same in squash as in tennis, as do forehand and backhand.

## Miscellaneous terminology

**The nick** Normally this refers to the spot where the wall joins the floor. A ball landing in the nick will rebound in an unpredictable manner, and may well just roll along the floor and become impossible to retrieve. Players therefore aim, whenever possible, to hit the nick, normally on the side walls.

**Turning** A somewhat controversial way of returning a ball in the rear of the court. A player is said to have 'turned' on the ball if he has, for example, aimed to volley a ball high on his backhand and either missed or refrained from playing the shot and has then followed the ball round and taken it on his forehand as it rebounds after hitting the side and rear walls. It is perfectly legal, but the controversy arises because it is liable to be an uncontrolled shot and there is a considerable risk of striking one's opponent, now presumably somewhere in the middle of the court and with nowhere to go to be safe. If a player cannot be sure that he will not hit his opponent he should not hit the ball, but should ask for a 'let' (q.v.).

**Mental turning** Similar to turning except that the player does not physically turn in order to follow the ball round. He remains standing facing the front wall and allows the ball to pass behind him via the side or rear wall, and plays it when it emerges on the centre of the court side of him. Again he should refrain from hitting the ball if there is the slightest danger of striking the opponent.

**Let** An undecided rally when it is fair to both players to restart it level. For example, if a ball breaks during play, if a player is obstructed in his efforts to get to the ball and the referee decides no one is to blame, if something falls into the court, or if the referee is unable to decide whether a ball was good or not.

**Match**   A match is normally the best of five games, each game being won by the player who first reaches nine points unless the game has been 'set'.

**Setting**   If the score reaches eight all, the player who is the receiver at that point has the option of choosing 'no set' or 'set two'. The former means that the game continues to 9 and someone wins it 9-8, while the latter means that the game continues to 10 and someone wins it 10-9 or 10-8.

**Penalty stroke**   A referee will award a penalty stroke when a player has been guilty of an infringement of the rules which would make it unfair on his opponent to restart the rally again level. He can award a penalty for obstruction, distraction, dangerous play, etc.

**Knock up** or **warm up**   This refers to the period prior to the game in which the players get the ball and themselves warmed up and ready to play. Normally the contestants will knock up together, and if so they are allowed five minutes. However, either player can insist on a separate knock up, in which case they spin a racket for the right to choose who goes first, and in this case the player going first has $3\frac{1}{2}$ minutes and his opponent $2\frac{1}{2}$ minutes.

**Double hit**   For a shot to be legal, the racket must make one clean strike of the ball. It is illegal if the ball is 'carried' on the racket or hit twice. This includes the case where, close to a side wall, the racket has hit the ball against the wall, and then again on the follow through as it comes off the wall.

**Hand**   Until recently, the server was known as hand-in and the receiver as hand-out, but in the interests of simplification these have now been dropped. However, a hand is still

used to indicate a period of play during which one of the players retains the service. As the server continues to serve and score points while he is winning rallies, one can say for example 'A scored five points in his first hand'. When the receiver wins a rally and so takes over the right to serve, the marker will preface his call of the score with the words 'hand out'. As he always calls the servers points first, 3-2 would become 'hand out 2-3'.

**Scoring**   If a player has not scored, his 'total' is called 'love', while if the scores are level, the call is, for example, 'three all'.

**Marker's calls**   Fault; Foot fault; Not up; Down; One fault; Out; Hand out; No set; Set two; Game ball; Match ball. He also has to repeat all refereeing decisions and call the score.

**Referee's calls**   Stop; Time; Half-time; Yes let; No let; Stroke to A; Stroke to B.

# THE GAME – A GUIDE

**W**hilst the whole object of this book is to encourage people to play squash and to tell them how to do so, it would be irresponsible not to mention the risks players take. One would not advise would-be mountaineers to go and climb mountains without warning of the dangers ahead, and the safeguards necessary to avoid accidents. A cricket manual would emphasize the dangers of being hit by a rapidly moving object weighing $5\frac{1}{2}$ ounces, and describe the protective equipment available to minimize possible injuries. So, before we run through a typical game of squash, let us first explain the dangers to be avoided. Firstly, squash is an extremely energetic and demanding game, and any intense exercise is a strain on a body not used to it. Beginners are not usually at risk, because the fact that they are only beginners means that they are not yet sufficiently accomplished to sustain the long and arduous rallies that will ensue when they are able to keep the ball in play longer. Nevertheless, it would be foolish for anyone to try to play squash if they had any medical problems, such as a heart complaint or high blood pressure, or were considerably overweight. Squash is a great game for people wishing to keep fit, but there are risks in using it as a means of getting fit in the first place. Secondly, it is very stupid to try to do anything highly energetic immediately after eating a heavy meal or having a long session in the bar. Obviously individuals vary in this respect, but it really cannot be a good idea to go directly from a blow-out at the local Chinese or Tandoori to your squash club! Thirdly, squash rackets and balls can inflict very nasty injuries indeed, and it is absolutely essential that all players remember that they must not attempt to play a shot if there is the slightest risk of hitting their opponent with either ball or racket. The eye is particularly vulnerable. A ball just fits into the socket, and although the blow is painful, the damage is done as the ball rebounds and, in recovering its shape, sucks off and detaches the retina. This can happen with a relatively softly-hit ball, so the player should refrain from any shot where there is the remotest possibility of hitting his opponent, and start the rally again with a let. So remember the basic rules:

**1** Get fit to play squash, do not play squash to get fit.
**2** Be sensible about eating and drinking before playing.
**3** Never play a stroke if there is the remotest chance of injuring your opponent – squash *can* be a dangerous game!

*The forehand lob service. Note the position of the server: he is about to hit the ball from as far forward and as near the side wall as possible. The receiver is standing near the back wall and is watching the server to prevent being surprised by a fast service, and to be able to watch the ball from the moment it is hit.*

# RULES · OF · THE · GAME

The game is played by two players as 'singles' – there is not enough room for a doubles match. Most matches consist of the best of three or five games.

At the commencement of a game both players are normally allowed five minutes to warm up. In an organized game the referee will advise when $2\frac{1}{2}$ minutes have lapsed to enable the players to swap sides.

The object of a game of squash is to score more points than your opponent by forcing him or her to be unsuccessful in returning your shot. The first person to score 9 points is the winner but when the score is first called at 8-all the receiving player (i.e. the non-server) can have the game 'set'. This means that play continues until one player reaches 10. If he chooses this option the marker will call 'Eight all, set two'. If he does not ask for it to be set then 'no set' is declared by the marker ('Eight all, no set, game ball') and the first player to score 9 points is the winner.

You can only win points if you are the server. If you are the receiver and win the rally (known as the stroke), you do not get a point but become the server. If you win the next rally then you score a point.

Service in the first place is decided by the spin of the racket or the toss of a coin. Thereafter the server retains the right to serve until the receiver wins a stroke.

# SQUASH

At the commencement of the game the server can choose which service box he serves from, but thereafter all serves must be from alternate boxes until he loses the stroke. When service changes hands (hand out), the new server has the choice of service box.

When serving you should have the number '3' firmly fixed in your mind, because: (a) there are three things to get right in order that the service is good; (b) there are three ways of serving a single fault; and (c) there are three ways of serving your 'hand' out, a sort of 'instant double fault'.

The three things to remember for the service to be good are: (1) part of one foot at least must be entirely in the service box, in contact with the floor and not touching the line at the moment of striking the ball – if it is not, a foot fault is called. (2) For the service to be good the ball must be delivered from the hand directly to the racket (in other words you cannot bounce it off the wall or floor before serving), and struck directly towards front wall. The ball must then hit the front wall between the cut line and the out of court line. (3) It must then rebound so that it bounces on the floor in the back corner of the court opposite to the service box, provided the receiver does not volley it, which he may elect to do.

The three ways in which a single fault can be called are: (1) Having a foot fault called. (2) When the ball hits the front wall on or below the cut line (but provided it is above the board). (3) If the ball bounces on any part of the court other than in the opposite back-half of the court. Landing on the short

*The lob service from the backhand side of the court. The receiver watches the server attentively.*

line or half court line constitutes a fault.

The three 'double faults' are: (1) If the ball fails to reach the front wall above the board. (2) If the ball hits another wall on its way to the front wall. (3) If the ball is out of court on any wall or in the roof area.

The server is allowed one fault; a second fault results in service being passed to the opposing player. The receiver may take a fault on the first service, and if he does this makes the fault good and the rally is then in progress as normal.

Once the server has put the ball in play the rally continues with players alternately hitting the ball on to the front wall, either directly or via the side or back walls. The ball must hit the front wall between the board and out of court line. The ball is allowed to bounce once before it is played, but it can be volleyed, as in tennis.

The server's score is always read out first, so, if you won the first point of a game the score would be one-love. If you then lost the next stroke, service would pass to your

*The defensive service from the forehand side; the ball is struck near the centre of the court to narrow the angle on the front wall. Again, the receiver watches closely.*

opponent and the score would then be love-one. In an organized match the marker would, in such a case, declare: 'Hand out, love-one', thus indicating service had changed hands, followed by the score.

A one-minute rest between games is allowed in competitive squash, with two minutes if the match goes to a deciding fifth game. The extra minute is more than welcome on such an occasion!

The player who wins each game retains the right to serve first in the next game. And in this case he can serve from the same box as in the last service of the previous game.

Lets are quite often called in squash to resolve doubtful decisions, obstruction, etc. When a let is called the serve is replayed from the same service box as the original

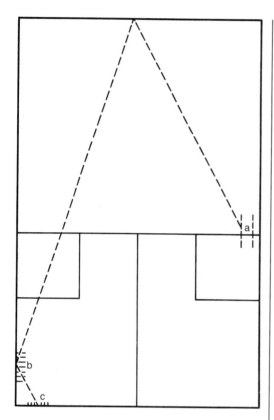

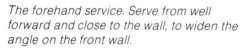

*The forehand service. Serve from well forward and close to the wall, to widen the angle on the front wall.*

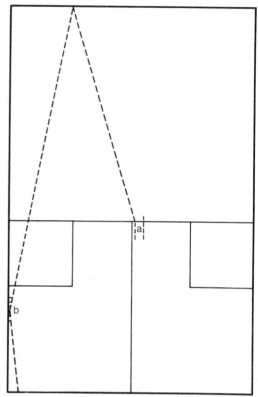

*A defensive service from the right court. Hit the ball towards the centre of the court to narrow the angle on the front wall.*

serve. In an organized game the referee will make such decisions on the players' behalf, but in a friendly game a let is often the best and easiest solution to any possible dispute.

It is never too early to learn the 'close contact' rules of squash. These are the rules designed to deal with the problems arising from the fact that both players are in the same limited space, moving at high speed and swinging rackets. If there were no rules indicating how players should move around the court, and what they must do and not do, the chaos that would result would be similar to what could happen on the roads if

there were no Highway Code. Even in friendly games, the players should be aware, for their own safety, what they may and may not do, and certainly by the time they reach the stage of having their games refereed, they will need to know what offences a referee is looking for and what penalties they are likely to get if they transgress. The rules have two main aims: the first is the safety of the players and the second is to ensure that each player has a fair chance to play his game unhampered by an obstructive opponent. Let us then look in detail at these 'close contact' rules. After all, in many ways they are the most important in squash.

Geoff Hunt, arguably the
best player out of the back
corners and off the back
wall.

## THE · CLOSE · CONTACT · RULES

The basis of correct movement in a squash court is contained in Rule 12. This rule requires a player, when he has finished his shot, to 'make every effort' to move away in order to give his opponent a fair view of the ball, a direct run to it, freedom to play the shot of his choice at it and freedom to hit the ball directly to the front wall or the side walls near the front wall. If the referee does not consider that a player has 'made every effort', he is required to award a penalty stroke to his opponent. However, even if a player is making every effort, he can still be penalized if nevertheless he prevents a likely winning shot.

For example, if you play a good drop shot and your opponent can only just scrape it up at full stretch, the ball may return close to your opponent, who is totally off balance and unable to move clear. You are just behind him and if you could get at the ball you would be bound to play a winner to the rear of the court, but your opponent is quite inadvertently and unintentionally blocking the shot. Obviously it would be unfair on you to restart the rally again with a let, so the referee will award the stroke to you. The thinking behind this is that that is the fair result to the rally and therefore the referee must give the stroke to you.

Sometimes it may appear that a player is unlucky to be penalized, but one has to analyse how a situation 'built up' and who

*After playing his shot back into his 'slice of cake', the player must exit via the centre of the court route, rather than straight to the T.*

was responsible for it. A bad referee takes a mental photograph of the end of the situation, while a good referee is re-running his mental video to see what had gone before.

I think there are two very important points here that you should bear in mind every time you think you are entitled to a let or a penalty stroke. The first is that your opponent is where he is in the court as a result of your previous shot; if you hit the ball into the front forehand corner, for example, your opponent has to go there in order to play his next stroke, so you cannot blame him for being there or for exploiting any advantage he gets from being in that position. Secondly, every time you hit the ball, unless your opponent is kind enough to hit it back to you in the centre of the court, you will be in one of the four quarters of the court.

Let us, as an example, assume you are a right-handed player having to play the ball in the rear backhand quarter of the court. We have already said the T area in the centre of the court is the place from which to dominate the court, and you should try to get back to the T after every shot. So you have four choices: you may opt for the drop shot or reverse angle which will take the ball into the front backhand quarter of the court; you may choose the angle or crosscourt drop which will take it into the front forehand quarter, or the cross court drive or lob, which will take it into the rear forehand quarter. If you play any of these, you are free to move directly, by the shortest route, back to the T, because you will have made it necessary for your opponent to move away from the T to fetch the ball, and so there is no risk of a collision.

However, if for your own advantage you choose the fourth option, which is to drive or lob the ball down the backhand side wall so that it returns to the same quarter of the court from which you played the ball, you have to accept the responsibilities that go with the advantages you hope to gain. You

have, so to speak, created a 'slice of cake', from the T to the side wall, and from the T to about halfway along the back wall. This is now territory that belongs to your opponent, and represents the area in which he may wish to play the ball. Remember, he is entitled to play the shot of his choice, and this covers the rapid movement to cut the ball off early, and the delayed stroke as it rebounds from the rear wall. He must be given complete freedom to do either, or anything in between.

Now you may not move directly back to the T as he will be moving right up the centre of the slice of cake, and if any collision or distraction results, you will be penalized, because you have not made every effort to give your opponent the unhindered progress to the ball to which he is entitled. You must move sideways as quickly as possible and then, once you are out of the 'slice' move up to the T. The same applies in the front quarters of the court.

If you have to play the ball from a position in one of the front corners, you do not have to play a drop or reverse angle which will return the ball into that corner; any other shot will enable you to run straight back to the T, but the drop or reverse angle require the immediate sideways movement out of the 'slice' before you start moving back to the T. The point is that the referee's mental video may reveal that a collision situation has come about as a result of your wrong choice of shot rather than your opponent's awkwardness. You should therefore think carefully about the results of a shot you are considering as you approach the ball, and whether it is more likely to land you in trouble than some of the other possible shots.

Rule 12 has now been expanded to include this sort of thinking. Up to now, as has been explained so far, all the requirements have been directed at the player who has just played his shot, i.e. the 'outgoing striker', and the 'incoming striker' could – and all too frequently did – claim a let when only slightly impeded, with the result that a very large number of rallies ended in lets, and the game was becalmed. The more ruthless players, when tired, could normally engineer a let in order to get a break. This resulted in highly unattractive and very boring squash, and in an endeavour to combat this, two new concepts have been added to Rule 12.

## Amendments to Rule 12

Firstly, the incoming striker is now required to get to and play the ball if at all possible. Even if he is slightly impeded, and it means brushing past his opponent to do so, he must now try to keep the rally going. His appeal for a let will be turned down if the referee does not feel he has made the required effort to keep the rally going. Secondly, the idea of 'creating one's own

interference' has been introduced. The whole object of 'strengthening' the rule was, as I have explained, to put an end to the repeated let situation, which was making the game very boring and unattractive, with particularly unfortunate effects on sponsors and would-be television presenters. In England, the concept of 'creating one's own interference' was interpreted as meaning that a player who played a bad shot, or put himself in a poor position as a result of wrong anticipation, could deny himself the right to a fair view of the ball or a direct line to it, would have to redeem his error by running round his opponent, and would not get a let by simply running into him. Unfortunately, other countries did not

*A has played a bad shot back to himself and must give B complete freedom to play the probable angle winner.*

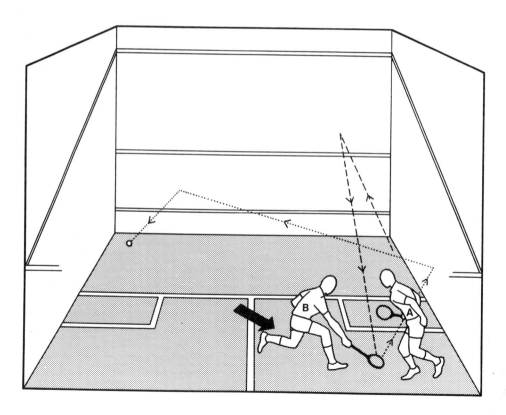

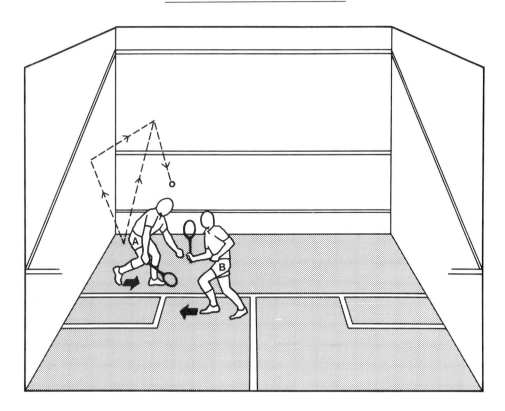

*A has played a bad shot which is returning on a line between himself and the T. He must not cross that line if, in doing so, he is obstructing B's view of the approaching ball or his shot at it. Stroke to B.*

interpret things in quite the same way, and the ISRF have ruled that 'created interference' refers only to the rare situations where a player does have a direct line to the ball, but does not take it, and collides with his opponent quite unnecessarily. In all other situations, however poor his previous shot and however faulty his anticipation, a player can still claim a let if he does not have a direct line to the ball. Hopefully, the English interpretation will eventually be approved, as it obviously leads to a much fairer outcome to the rally. In the meantime, however, the only solution to continual lets would seem to be a much stricter interpretation of the rule,

which requires the outgoing striker to 'make every effort' to move clear after playing his shot. In general, referees are far too lenient over this and the lets remain too frequent.

So to sum up the rule in brief:

**1** The outgoing striker must make every effort to move clear at once, via the centre of the court route if necessary, in order to give his opponent a fair view of the ball, a direct run to it, complete freedom of stroke, and freedom to hit the ball directly to the front wall or side walls near the front wall.

**2** The outgoing striker may still be penalized – even if he has made every effort – if he obstructs a likely winning stroke.

**3** The incoming striker must convince the referee that he can get to the ball and is making every effort to do so and to play it whenever possible.

**4** A player will not get a let if he has created his own interference.

## Player struck by the ball

The next of the close contact rules that should be clearly understood is what happens when the ball strikes one of the players, as is inevitable within the close confines of a squash court. There are several ways in which this can happen.

Let us look first at what happens when

*Top left: If only player B could get at the ball, he could play a winner, so he wins the point.*

*Bottom left: A no let situation – player B has come up on the wrong side of A, so he is not eligible for a let.*

*Below: B has struck A with what would have been a good return going directly to the front wall, Stroke to B.*

your shot hits your opponent on its way to the front wall. The basic rule says that if in the opinion of the referee, the ball would have gone directly to the front wall as a good return, you win the rally. If the referee considers that it would have been a good return but would have struck one of the other three walls on its way to the front wall, it is a let, and if the referee does not think the ball would have reached the front wall, your opponent wins the rally.

The reasoning behind these decisions is that in the first instance, your opponent is directly in your way and is not giving you freedom to hit the ball to the front wall, and so must pay the penalty for being out of position. In the second case, your opponent is giving you freedom to hit the ball to the front wall, but he has to be somewhere in the court, and cannot be expected to keep clear of all possible angle shots you may select to

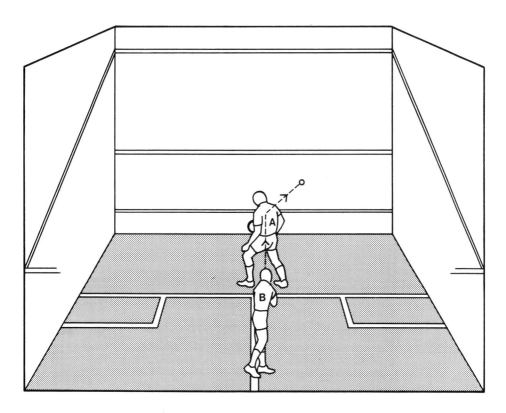

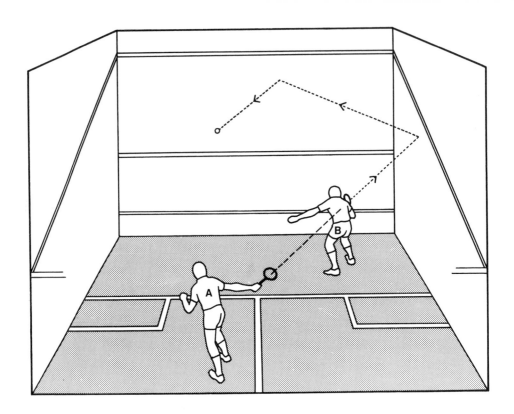

hit – or mis-hit! In the third case, you have failed to make a good return, so must lose the rally.

There are three exceptions to this basic rule. The first two cover cases where the ball is in fact going directly to the front wall as a good return, but the decision is that it is only a let, instead of a stroke to you.

The first exception occurs when there is a second attempt to hit the ball. Let us assume that you have already played at and missed the ball. Maybe you slipped or just could not reach it – in any event, you played a shot at it and did not make contact. However, you recovered very quickly and chased after the ball, and caught up with it in time to play a second shot, this time successfully. Now however, your opponent is in the line of fire and is hit by the ball (or you refrain from playing it for fear of hitting your opponent). In either event, this is a let, because your opponent was perfectly clear of your first attempt and can hardly be expected to anticipate that you would miss it, and so is

*In both these cases (above and right) a let is played, as A's return would have been good had they not struck B.*

*Bottom right: A has hit B with what would have been a good return but going up via the back wall. A let is played.*

not to blame for being in the line of fire of a second go.

The second exception occurs when you 'turn' on the ball. This means that you have either played and missed or refrained from playing, a ball, normally in one of the back corners, and have then followed it round as it hits the side and back wall, and have then taken it on the forehand in the backhand rear quarter of the court, or vice versa. If you then hit your opponent, now standing in the centre of the court somewhere, it is only a let, on the grounds that this is likely to be an uncontrolled 'swipe' by you, desperate to return the ball somehow. Your opponent

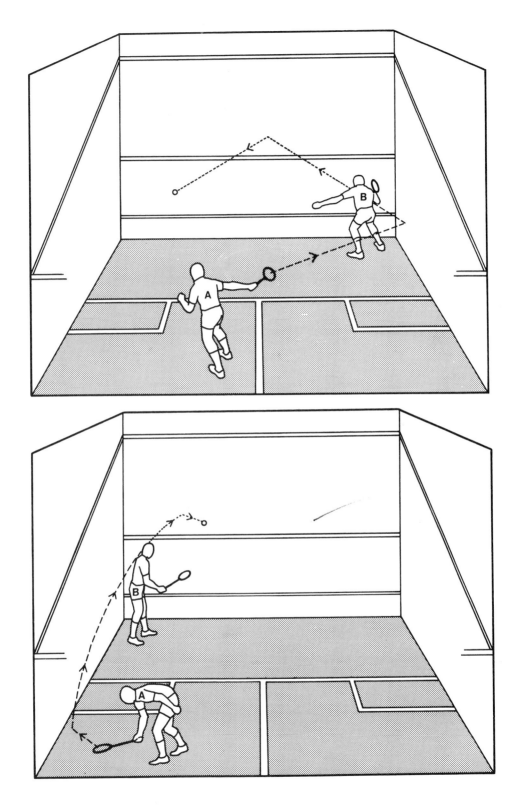

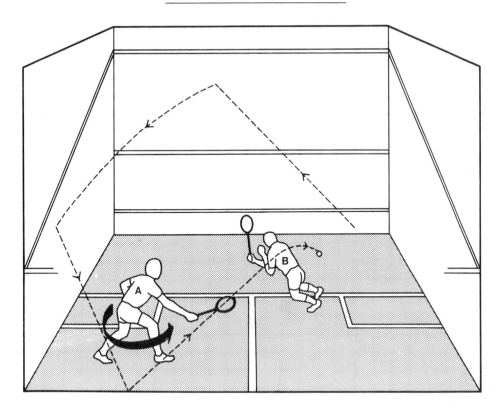

cannot possibly anticipate where it will go, and so there is no safe place for him to go to avoid being hit. Of course, we come back to the point that whilst it is perfectly legal to 'turn' on the ball, you ought not to play it if there is any risk of hitting your opponent, and if you were to continue to hit the ball close to your opponent in this sort of situation, the referee would soon warn you for dangerous play.

Allied to this is the case of 'mental turning'. This means that you do not actually physically turn, but allow the ball to pass round behind you and then catch up with it as it re-emerges on the other side of your

**The speed of the game dictates that even the best players sometimes get their feet in the wrong positions. Here Jonah Barrington is caught in a very uncharacteristic pose!**

*A has hit B after 'turning', so that even though the ball was going directly to the front wall, a let is played.*

body. The problem is the same; you will not be absolutely sure when you will hit the ball, or where it will go, so your poor opponent certainly cannot tell, and it would be unfair to penalize him for being hit. However, whilst your opponent cannot lose the rally if hit, it should be borne in mind that he is not totally blameless. You cannot possibly turn if his initial stroke is close to the side wall or to a good length at the back of the court; there would just not be room for you to get the other side of it. Certainly if you turn, and can see where your opponent is and can see the chance of a winner into an open area in the court, you are fully entitled to try it – you are only cashing in on a poor shot of your

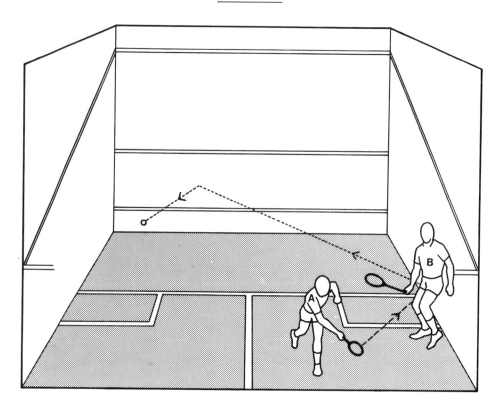

opponent. All you may not do is play a shot which puts your opponent at risk.

The final exception to the basic rule arises in a situation where you hit your opponent with some form of angle or boast, going to the front wall as a correct return, but via one of the other walls. This is normally only a let, but to prevent the more ruthless players deliberately getting in the way of angles likely to cause them problems, an addition has been made to this part of the rule, which says that the referee may award a stroke to a player if he considers that a likely winning shot has been intercepted.

This normally occurs when a player in the back corner of the court hits a poor shot back towards himself. His opponent comes from the T to play the ball, and with the original player trapped in the corner, the obvious winner is the angle towards the opposite front corner. The player must give

*A has hit B with what would have been a winning shot, so A is awarded the stroke.*

his opponent freedom to attempt this, and not sidle up to the wall, on the pretext of getting out of the way, thus covering the very part of the side wall that the winning angle would need to hit.

So much for players being hit by the ball on its way to the front wall. Let us now consider what the rules say about the ball striking a player as it returns from that wall. There are obviously two situations, one when your opponent's stroke hits you (and vice versa) and the other, when your own shot returns and strikes you. Basically, the rule says that a player hit in this way loses the rally, but we again return to the referee's golden rule about achieving a fair result for each rally, and there are occasions when it would not be fair to interpret the rule as simply as that.

Normally if your shot returns and hits your opponent, it is your stroke, on the grounds that your opponent has not got his racket in position in time and must pay the penalty. However, there are occasions when this would not be a fair decision. For example, if you had been standing in front of your opponent and mis-hit the ball back directly towards yourself, and just managed to leap clear at the last moment, so that the ball went on and hit your opponent. The referee would argue in this case that your opponent had not had a fair view of the approaching ball and should therefore not be penalized. He would award at least a let, and, depending on the circumstances, could even award him the stroke on the grounds of your obstruction.

A similar situation can arise, usually close to a side wall, when you hit the ball hard towards your opponent, who is between you and the side wall. He sees it coming and tries to step out of its way and give himself room to play it. However, he finds that you are close to him and he is unable to move clear of the approaching ball, which hits him. Again, the referee would feel that this was your fault and it would not be fair for your opponent to lose that rally.

The same sort of thinking applies to the occasions when your own shot returns from the front wall and hits you. Normally you are just paying the penalty for a poor shot and bad positioning, and deserve to lose the rally. However, this would not be fair if your

*A hits B with the ball as it rebounds from the front wall and wins the rally.*

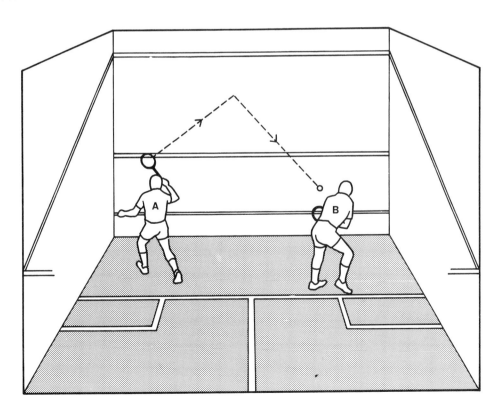

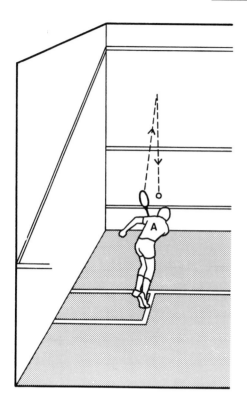 

*A hits himself with the ball and loses the rally. B hits himself with the ball because A is preventing him from moving clear, and a let is played.*

opponent had contributed to the situation. An example of this would again be where you are trapped by your opponent's position close to you which prevents you from moving clear of the approaching ball. Similarly, if you have hit the ball from the rear of the court back towards yourself, and your opponent in front of you shapes as if to play the ball, but then lets it go through with the intention of taking it later, probably off the back wall, and it hits you, that would also only be a let.

So the close contact rules are safety regulations, intended to eliminate injury by keeping the players well apart, while at the same time giving both an equal chance of playing their game unimpeded and unhindered.

# MARKING · & · REFEREEING

As I have already mentioned, once you reach a level of play that merits inclusion in a club side, or reach the later stages of an internal tournament, you must expect to find one or preferably two officials in charge of every match. Some sort of arbiter is particularly important in squash for a number of reasons.

In the first place the ball is small and moves at great speed, and it is not always easy to see whether it has just touched the top of the board or the bottom of the out of court line or not. When the result is uncertain it is obviously better for everyone if a neutral eye makes the decision.

Secondly, most of the controversial situations occur when one player gets in the way of his opponent. Normally, he will not be able to see round his opponent clearly enough to know whether he is entitled to a let, or whether it was an outright winner and he was unable to get near it, or even whether it was a very poor shot and he should be given a penalty stroke.

Similarly, your opponent, not having eyes in the back of his head, will have no idea how near to you he is, or how fast and along which line you are approaching. So the only solution, in games where there is no official, has to be a let, and the rally must be replayed. This is clearly unsatisfactory, and after a while, it is common for one of the players to begin to feel he is getting something of a raw deal, and all the lets are rather less than just. He will hopefully accept the decisions of a 'neutral' on the balcony with a clear view of both players and the ball.

There are two other considerations. Firstly, once you have reached a level at which your matches are being marked and refereed, you will find that you are expected to act as marker and referee for your team mates' matches. You must therefore know what the officials are expected to say and do, not only as a player, but when you have to take your turn at actually doing the job.

Secondly, if marking and refereeing are taught alongside normal playing coaching, more people can be involved. This is an important factor for coaches in charge of large groups. It means they can not only occupy two pupils on a court but two others as well, acting as marker and referee in the gallery. At half-time they should of course change over.

So far, we have only mentioned that the officials are known as the marker and the referee, and given a very brief outline of their duties and how one person can take charge of a match by carrying out both roles simultaneously. Let us now look in more detail at the way they are expected to act.

The marker is the 'voice' that keeps the game flowing, by making the appropriate calls and by announcing the score. Until quite recently, most squash players in the world spoke English, even if frequently with a foreign accent. Nowadays, as many as twenty different countries may send representatives to the European championships alone, and the game has also spread to many other countries in Africa, South America and Asia. It is therefore not unusual to find players who do not have English as their first, or even second, language. Because English has always been the language of squash, they will understand enough to follow the marker and referee if they make their announcements in the accepted way, but not if they go off into some strange version of their own. It is vitally important therefore to stick to the calls recognized and approved by the International Federation, and to make sure that the normal procedures are adhered to.

## Markers' calls

Before embarking on details, it is worth pointing out that the marker and referee have to walk a tightrope. It is necessary to strike the right balance between carrying out their tasks efficiently and imposing themselves too much on the game. It is not unusual for inexperienced officials to get carried away with the power they now have and virtually 'take over' the match. They forget that they are only 'extras' to the principal actors, albeit very necessary extras, but the principal actors are the players and it is, and must remain, their game.

The marker has the difficult task of ensuring that he is audible, not only to the players but to everyone watching the game as well. He must therefore be loud enough to compete with competition from neighbouring courts, without giving the impression that he is trying to dominate proceedings. It is not an easy job, especially as the majority of people shrink from any form of public speaking. Similarly the referee must remember that, as his title makes clear, he is basically there to be referred to in cases of doubt or disagreement. He is not there to impose his views on the rules on two players who are perfectly happy with their game. He *is* there, however, to ensure that a fair result is arrived at and to ensure that neither player at any stage or in any way gains an unfair advantage. So he may emerge from his position of merely dealing with appeals and impose decisions on the players only when he feels that this is necessary to get the fair outcome to a rally. Both officials must be courteous to the players and try to give the impression that they are there to help the players have a good and enjoyable game. Let us now consider the details of the marker's duties.

He must be clear in all his calls, and these must be the recognized and orthodox calls, approved by the International Federation, and accepted by players throughout the world. He must learn by experience to make them quickly and never hold up play, and if he has been doing a lot of marking and refereeing on his own, i.e. a one official situation with the two hats, he must remember that when he is working with a referee, he himself makes no decisions on lets or penalties, but must wait for his colleague to tell everyone what the decision is.

His adherence to the correct calls is vital. Not only is that the only way he can be sure that both players fully understand what is going on, but his correctness or the reverse has an effect on the players. It may well be unfair, but it is only human nature, for the players to tend to judge the referee by the marker. If the calls are clear, quick and correct, they will assume that the game is in good hands and the referee is probably all right as well. Whereas if the marker is slow and incorrect, the players will assume that

the referee is equally incompetent, and will appeal, dissent and so on, and the game can quickly disintegrate into a shambles.

The first call the marker will make is the introduction to the match. This always should come in a set format, which if correct will give the players confidence. Begin by announcing the match, if it is worth announcing. One does not say, for example, 'Fourth string match in the third team match in the nineteenth division of the West Rutland League', but one does say, 'Final of the Surrey closed championship', or even 'Semi-final of the club championship'. This is followed by the names of the two players and who is which in four words, e.g. 'Smith serving, Jones receiving'; then the terms of the match, 'Best of five games', if it is (some tournaments have to cut down to best of three games in order to get the event through in time) and then the score, which at that moment is 'Love all'.

The last match in the 1986 open championship was announced as follows: 'Final of the (sponsor's name) British Open Championship, Khan serving, Norman receiving, best of five games, love all'. In an event like that, there will have been further 'introductions' by a compère with a microphone, before and during the knock up period, giving the life history and recent results of the players, where they come from and who they have beaten *en route* to the final. Even so, after the referee has brought the knock up to an end, the marker will make the official introduction to the match in the terms given above, when both players are ready to start.

The only variation to this format is when it is a team event, when the marker may say, 'Smith, Yorkshire, serving, Jones, Lancashire, receiving', in order to help spectators follow the team fortunes as well as the individual

**Jansher Khan, world number one in 1987. He took the crown from the brilliant Jahangir Khan, but will his talent prove as durable?**

# SQUASH

players. During the match, he must use the following calls on the occasions explained.

**Foot fault**   The marker must call this loud and clear, at the moment the server strikes the ball if he does not have at least one foot correctly grounded within the service box. The whole word is called, rather than just 'Fault', in order to give the server the reason why he has been 'called', and because as the service is only just on its way to the front wall, the extra syllable does not matter much.

**Fault**   This is called the moment the service becomes a fault, i.e. when the ball strikes the cut line or the lower panel on the front wall, or bounces anywhere but within the opposite back corner of the court. The fault calls must be made as early as possible in order to give the receiver as much time as possible to decide whether he wishes to take the ball or not. The rules allow him this slight advantage in the event of his opponent's minor error, and the marker must ensure that he gets it. A late call denies him the advantage, and can often lead to a complete mis-hit if the receiver hears it just as he is about to play the ball because he has not yet heard that it was a fault. Sometimes, of course, the marker has to wait for the ball to bounce before he can call, and so cannot give the receiver such warning, but the aim must be to call all faults as early as possible.

**Not up**   This term is used to indicate any form of incorrect stroke, except for a ball that goes out of court. It immediately brings the rally to an end, but the marker must only call a ball 'not up' if he is convinced beyond any doubt at all that it was so. If he is in any doubt, he must allow play to continue, and if the player of the doubtful shot wins it, the opponent may then appeal to the referee for a ruling on that shot. This also applies to those occasions when the marker is considering calling 'down' or 'out'.

**Down**   The marker will call this when a player has hit the ball too low down on the front wall, i.e. his shot has hit the tin or board. 'Not up' would be an equally correct

call for such a shot, but there are occasions when a player can only barely reach a ball in the front of the court, and the resulting 'scrape' hits the ball very close to the top of the board. In order to make it clear to both players and spectators why he is stopping the rally, the marker should call 'Not up' if he is alleging that the player did not get the ball up before it bounced for the second time on the floor, and 'Down' if it was too low on the front wall.

**Out**   Called by the marker when he is sure the ball is out of court.

**Hand out**   This call is used by the marker prior to his call of the score when the service has changed hands. If, for example, the server has served at 3-2, but has lost the rally, the marker will announce the new score as 'Hand out, 2-3', because he is always required to call the server's points first.

**Score**   Between every rally, the marker must at least call the score, whatever else he is required to call. He calls the server's points first and if the scores are equal calls 'all' and if one player has not scored calls 'love'.

**One fault**   This is a call which the marker will add to his announcement of the score when the server is about to serve again after the receiver has elected not to play his previous service, which was a foot fault or fault. The marker will therefore call, for example, '3-2, one fault'. This makes it quite clear to the server that he is serving again with a fault registered against him, and not because his opponent was not ready, or for anything else which would mean that he was serving with a clean slate. The marker must remember to call 'one fault' again after the score if the next, and any subsequent, rallies end in 'lets'.

**Yes let; No let; Stroke to Smith**   These are refereeing decisions which the marker is required to repeat before announcing the new score resulting from such decisions. He should not try to repeat any words of warning or explanation by the referee to either or both players, but must repeat the actual decision. The referee should have made the decision clear to the players, so the marker must tell the spectators what the decision is.

**No set; Set two**   The marker adds these two calls to the score when it is 8-all, and the receiver has just indicated which of the two he has chosen. So, when the server wins the rally at 7-8, the marker announces 8-all. The receiver chooses to continue to play up to nine (no set) or to go on to ten (set two). The marker then calls '8-all, no set, game or match ball', or '8-all, set two'. However long the game continues after that, the marker does not repeat these calls. Having made the decision clear once, it is left to the presence or absence of 'game' or 'match' ball to clarify the situation.

**Game ball; Match ball**   Calls which the marker adds to the score when the server needs only to win the next rally to win the game or the match. When he may be about to win the match, only 'match ball' is called, although it is obviously also 'game ball' – the marker does not call both.

**New game**   After the referee has announced the end of the permitted rest period between games, the marker should introduce the new game, with the server's score first as usual, as follows: 'One game to love, love all' or 'Two games all, love all', etc. Having given the players' names and who is which in his initial introduction, he need not announce them again, but if he feels it would be helpful to any newcomers in the gallery, he may say 'Smith leads by two games to one, love all', etc.

**Order**   A newcomer to the marking scene may find these calls confusing and not know in what order to call them. It will help if he thinks of them in three groups and the order is then simply common sense.

The first group are things which affect the score, and are a sort of pre-explanation of the score he is about to announce. After all, not up, down or out indicate that one of the players has lost the rally and that will certainly affect the score. So will a

refereeing decision, and the call of hand out explains in advance why it is now 2-3 and not 3-2.

The second group is formed by the words of the actual score, 3-2, 8-1 etc., and the third group is the list of 'comments' on the score. They do not affect the score but are reminders of some fact to the players. For example, 'one fault' reminds the server that another fault will result in his losing the service. 'Game ball' and 'match ball' are reminders of the state of the match, in particular to the receiver, as they tell him that somehow he has got to win the coming rally, and 'no set' and 'set two' do not affect the fact that the score is 8-all, they merely inform everyone of what is going to happen next.

The referee is also now obliged to make certain calls, all of which are to do with his role as time keeper. He is required to call 'half-time' at the middle point of the knock up period, and 'time' at the end of the full five minutes. Similarly, in the interval between games, he must call 'Fifteen seconds', when only a quarter of a minute of the rest period remains, and 'Time' when it has expired completely. Both officials may call 'Stop' at any time, when they want the players to cease playing. This may be because they have not heard a marker's call which should have stopped the rally, or it could be for reasons of safety – perhaps someone has opened the court door or dropped a programme into the court, either of which could produce a serious injury to an unsuspecting player.

## Duties of the referee

We have already stressed that the referee is there for the purpose of getting the fair result to the match, by getting the fair result to each rally. And in order to achieve this, he is in complete charge of anything that could affect that result. He is the sole arbiter of whether the ball is satisfactory, the players' clothes conform with the rules, and are not distracting, the court is safe and acceptable and the behaviour of the spectators is not putting unfair pressure on either or both players. All appeals from the players go directly to him and they have no right of appeal against any decision he gives. He is therefore the 'senior partner' of the two officials.

One of his duties is to ensure that the players adhere strictly to the rules governing times, and he is responsible for calling 'Half-time' and 'Time' during and at the end of the knock-up, and 'Fifteen seconds' and 'Time' during and at the end of the rest periods between games. These apart, all other calls are made by the marker, except that either official may call 'stop' to bring a rally to an end, often when there is some element of danger if they were to play on.

Before a match he should ensure that he has a spare supply of balls in case of breakage, a watch with a second hand and adequate pens and paper for writing down the score. He should ensure that he and his marker are in position before the players come on court and must if necessary ensure that his marker is not delaying play or putting the players off in any way. When appealed to, he must answer the players direct, and may at any time, if he feels it would be helpful, warn either player or both, or explain a decision, in order to keep the game flowing safely and fairly.

Both officials must write down the score. There are a number of ways of doing this, but one of the most satisfactory (which can be done on any piece of paper and does not require a special pad) is to make two columns with the players names at the top, and write the score and side from which he is serving under the server's name.

**Lucy Soutter in the correct position for a backhand.**

# RULES CLINIC

Inevitably, you are bound to find yourself in situations not covered by the rules in the previous chapter. The Rules Clinic will, hopefully, clear up the more common disputes that arise during a game.

**If a player serves a foot fault, and the receiver does not take it, and the second service is a fault because it hits the lower half of the front wall, is that a 'double fault' situation?**

Yes. Any two consecutive single faults automatically lose the server his right to serve, whatever type of single faults are involved.

**In tennis, if the ball hits the top of the net and then falls into the opposite court, it is still in play. Is there an equivalent to the net-cord shot in squash?**

No. The moment a ball touches the top of the board the rally is over and the player who hit that shot has lost it, even if the ball then proceeds to go on and hit the front wall. Similarly, if the ball touches your opponent, or any part of his clothing or racket, the rally ends at that moment, even if the ball subsequently carries to the front wall. The referee has to make his decision under the rule governing 'striking the opponent with the ball'.

**If a player mis-hits the ball against the front wall so that it returns through his legs, or he is forced to jump over it, does he lose the rally?**

No – he may even win it, if his opponent is too far away to get to the ball. He only loses the rally if it actually touches him, his clothing or his racket. If his opponent is immediately behind him at the time, he is likely to lose the rally immediately afterwards under the 'striking the opponent' rule.

**If a player throws the ball up to serve, and then decides not to play the ball and allows it to drop on the floor, is that any sort of fault?**

No. As in tennis, if a player does not like his 'throw-up', he need not actually serve, and can restart without any penalty.

**Can the service be overarm or underarm?**

Yes. There is absolutely no restriction on the service action – i.e. overarm, underarm, forehand or backhand, provided the basic rule about the ball being struck directly after being propelled into the air by the non-racket hand is obeyed.

### What happens if a ball breaks during a game? Does the player who played the previous shot win the rally?

No. If the rally was still in progress when it broke, both players would still have an equal chance of winning it, so it is obviously fair to start it again, and the referee allows a let.

### If a player breaks his racket, or his shoe comes to pieces during a rally, is he entitled to a let?

No. A player is held to be responsible for supplying himself with efficient equipment which will not let him down, and if the rally ends because something of his has broken, sadly he loses the rally. Of course there are possible exceptions, if his opponent has contributed to the breakage, i.e. if the player had tripped over his opponent, and as a result had fallen and smashed his racket on the wall or floor, or if a shoe had broken because the opponent had inadvertently trodden on his foot, and he could not wrench his foot clear. In these cases a let would be allowed.

### What happens when some loud noise off court, such as a car backfiring in the car park outside, a baby screaming in the gallery or a glass being dropped and breaking, results in a player being distracted as he plays the ball? Is he entitled to a let?

Yes. It is obviously not a fair result to the rally if a player loses it because he has been put off at the vital moment of playing his stroke. The referee has to decide whether an incorrect shot, which appears to have lost the rally, was in fact genuinely caused by the distraction, and if so he will allow the let.

### A player hits the ball into the tin, but strikes his opponent on the follow through? Can he claim a let?

No. He played the ball unhindered, and so must stand by the result of his stroke, i.e. it is 'down' and he has lost the rally. The contact only occurred after the ball had been struck, and so had no effect on the actual shot. It is a different matter if a player strikes his opponent on his backswing as he prepares to play a normal stroke. The referee would then certainly allow at least a let, and quite possibly give the player a penalty stroke, if his opponent had been too close.

### On trying to change direction in the front of the court, a player trips over some gear of his opponent, left against the tin in one of the corners. Is he entitled to a let?

Yes, but the referee should have ensured that no kit is left in the court before the game started.

### At the end of a rally, the players decide that the server served from the wrong side. Is that rally replayed?

No, the result of the rally stands, but the server now serves from the other side, as though he had been correct. For example, if he has served wrongly from the right, he wins the rally and scores his point, but must now serve from the left.

### If a player misses the ball because it has rebounded oddly as a result of hitting a hole in the plaster, or a protruding door handle etc, is he allowed a let?

No, it is just bad luck. Once the game has begun both players accept the conditions – bad plaster, protruding door handles, etc., and both have an equal chance of being lucky or unlucky. A let would only be allowed if something unforeseen happened, such as a light suddenly going out during a rally, or a hitherto normal floorboard giving way just as a player put his weight on it.

**Is a player allowed to transfer his racket to his other hand, so that he plays every shot on the forehand, partially left and partially right-handed?**

Yes, he is fully entitled to do this.

**Is a player allowed to receive advice from his coach during a match?**

He may do so by meeting him outside the court in the intervals between games, but a coach must give no audible coaching from the gallery during a game, as this could be most distracting to the opponent. There can of course be no objection to prearranged signals, e.g. if the coach crosses his legs, it could mean 'lob more' etc. Such signals would be meaningless and therefore not distracting to the opponent.

**If a player is doubtful about his opponent's shot, should he point to it in order to draw the referee's attention to it, and to give advance notice that if he loses the rally, he will appeal?**

No. This practice is completely unacceptable. The referee will have noted the shot anyway and will be prepared to allow a let on the appeal if he was himself in any doubt about it. Pointing can only be distracting to an opponent, who may well lose the rally as a result of going for some over-ambitious winner because he knows his opponent will appeal if he loses the rally.

**If I serve and the ball goes below the cut line and then bounces in the front half of the court, have I committed one or two faults?**

You have committed two, but they only count as one.

**What happens if a player serves from the wrong box?**

If the receiver is aware of the fact and makes no attempt to return the ball he can ask the player to serve again but from the correct box.

**As the receiver, do I have to wait for the serve to hit the ground first before returning it?**

No, you can volley it, even if it was going to be a fault. But once you have played it you have condoned the serve and the ball is legally in play.

**Can the receiver therefore attempt to return any serve, whether it is a fault or not?**

Yes. If he does return a serve that is a fault then the serve is deemed to be good. However, he can only attempt to return the first service fault, he cannot play the second service fault, which is an automatic double fault, and a hand out situation.

# TECHNIQUE

S quash presents a rather different set of environmental and tactical problems from tennis. In tennis, a really hard shot over the net can go past an opponent, and the ball can be made to spin disconcertingly on landing if the racket slices across it at the moment of contact. Such subtleties do not apply in squash, because the first contact of the ball is against the front wall which removes all spin and takes much of the speed off it. However, the walls themselves cause problems not met in tennis.

It is obviously more difficult to hit a ball from a position very close to a side wall or near the back wall than from one in the middle of the court. The aim during a rally therefore must be to put your opponent under pressure by keeping the ball close to the walls and to 'a good length'. A good length means that the ball is going to bounce for the second time just before or just after it reaches the back wall, and so presents your opponent with a decision as to whether to have a hasty jab at it before it gets to the wall, or leave it to hit the wall, and hope it will rebound far enough to be retrievable.

It is therefore desirable to put pressure on your opponent by making him play the ball from a position close to a wall. Obviously the pressure is increased if he has to play it close to two walls, which means in the rear corners of the court. If the normal difficulties of a good length shot are added to by that shot also being very close to the side wall, it may not be possible for your opponent to return the ball at all, or if he does manage to

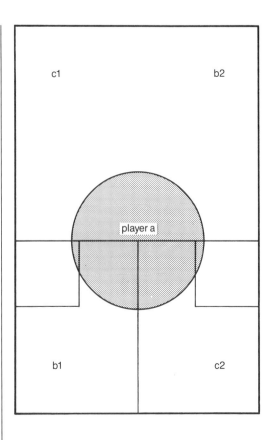

*The area covered by the 'oaktree' in the centre of the court, that is, the area a player can cover with his racket whilst standing on the T. The opponent should aim to play the ball short of it, past it down the side walls or over it into the near corners.*

do so it may be a very desperate 'scrape', which will present an easy winner in the front of the court. The most likely shots to produce this situation are the drive or lob down the nearest side wall, or the crosscourt lob, all of which can cause the maximum embarrassment in the rear corners.

Another aspect to remember is that a squash court is longer than it is broad. As a consequence, you can tire your opponent more quickly by making him run up and down it than by moving him from side to side. From the centre of the court position on the T, a player can reach the side walls in a couple of easy strides, but will have to do a bit more than that to get to a ball in one of the corners of the court. Ideally then, to achieve this, you should, for example, hit the ball into the back backhand corner, and as soon as possible place your next shot somehow into the front forehand corner. This may be a winner, or your opponent may be able to get to it, but even if he does, he will have had to cover the longest distance possible, and in time, if repeated, this should exhaust him.

We have already mentioned the importance of getting to the T as soon as possible after each shot, and it is perhaps helpful to imagine an oaktree, planted with its centre on the T and its circumference reaching to just inside the service boxes on each side. The tree is sawn off at about 3·6m (12ft) high and represents the area a player can reach with one foot still on the T. If therefore your shot returns from the front wall and hits the 'oaktree', you will probably lose the rally. The reason is that your opponent can now play the ball from the T, and if he is there, you must be somewhere else, i.e. in one of the four quarters of the court, and this gives the opportunity to your opponent to hit the ball into the corner of the court diametrically furthest away from that quarter.

The two points to be remembered from this are firstly, always to get back to the T as quickly as possible after every shot and so

'plant your oaktree', ready to take advantage of any poor shot by your opponent. Secondly, ensure that none of your own shots returns from the front wall and hits the tree your opponent has planted. This means putting the ball into the front corners short of the tree, passing it down the side walls, or lobbing the ball over it into the rear corners. What also follows from this is the need to be able to play the full range of shots. There is little point in forcing your opponent to hit a weak shot back to the centre of the court, from which a drop or angle or whatever would be a certain winner, if you cannot then play the required shot.

In squash, as in all racket games, there is a generally accepted best or orthodox way of playing the shots, and it makes good sense for a beginner to book a few lessons with a coach early on to get the basics right. However, if world champions of sport were only orthodox players, the record books would not be full of the innovative players whose natural talent has not been spoilt by orthodox coaching. No coach could ever have been responsible for people like Denis Compton in cricket, Muhammed Ali in boxing or Arnold Palmer in golf and many others. Basically, they were all very good technicians, but over and above that they were able to do things not to be found in any coaching manual, and which no coach would have tolerated, and it was these things that made them stand out above their contemporaries.

Perhaps one of the main reasons that this country has not produced a tennis player of any note since Fred Perry before the war is that our coaching has been too stereotyped and orthodox, and whilst that has probably made a lot of moderate players into quite good players, it has also made any potential 'superstar' into only a good player too. If therefore you find you have a natural ability to play some particular shot, you should not be worried if you are not playing it in quite the way your coach recommends. Provided it works, you should go on playing it, and only

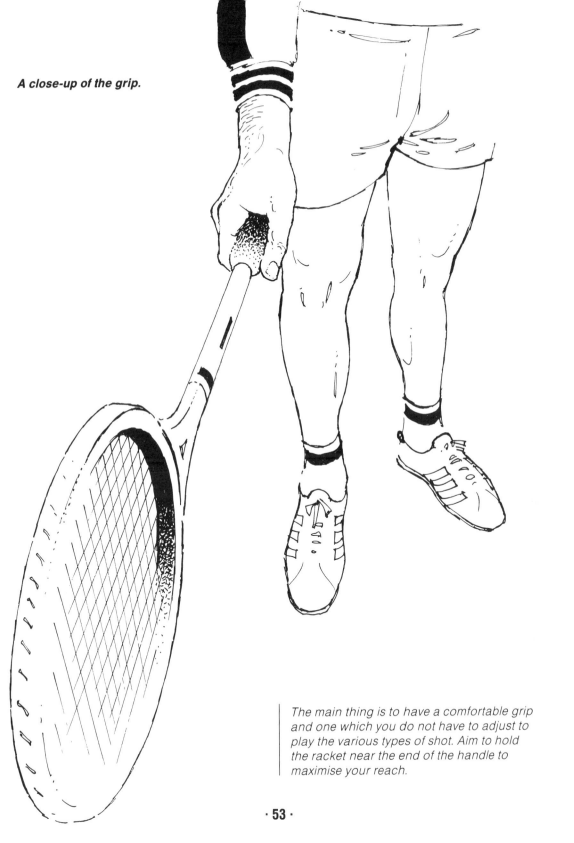

*A close-up of the grip.*

The main thing is to have a comfortable grip and one which you do not have to adjust to play the various types of shot. Aim to hold the racket near the end of the handle to maximise your reach.

*The backswing for the forehand: cock the wrist and keep your eye on the ball.*

*Strike the ball opposite the leading foot, with the racket horizontal.*

when it fails to produce results should you begin to analyse how it differs from the orthodox, and whether after all your coach may have a point.

## Grip

One comes up against this problem immediately when trying to give advice on how to grip the racket. Hashim Khan, the greatest player of all time, held the racket a long way up the shaft, almost beyond the end of the handle area. This of course reduced his reach (and he was not a tall man with long arms) but his quite incredible

speed about the court more than made up for this. The short grip also meant that he seldom had to 'boast' the ball out of the back corners, he could get behind the ball and whip it down the side wall.

The average player uses a racket with a normal handle and holds the racket towards the end of it. The actual material of the grip is entirely a matter of personal taste and choice. If you sweat a lot you will probably want a towelling grip and will just have to accept the fact that this will need changing at fairly frequent intervals. But you may find the leathery or rubbery grips more convenient. My only criterion for grip is that it

*Follow through upwards, not round.*

*The correct basic position for the backhand.*

should be comfortable, and not cause blisters every time you have a long match. It should also enable you to play all the shots, forehand and backhand, without having to change your grip – something you will not have time to do in a fast rally.

## Footwork

A similar approach applies to footwork. There is a genuinely accepted optimum way of producing strokes. On the forehand (for a right-handed player) you should ideally be facing the forehand side wall, with your leading left foot nearer to it than the right

and the weight moving forward on to it as the stroke is played. The reverse applies to the backhand, but the action is the same. The front foot is now the right foot and it should be slightly closer to the side wall than the left, and the weight transferred forward during the shot. The aim should be to strike the ball level with the front or leading foot, with your arm and racket more or less parallel with the floor, so that your wrist has the maximum opportunity to control the direction of the ball at the last moment. This applies to all the shots in the game, other than those which are designed to get the ball out of the back corner.

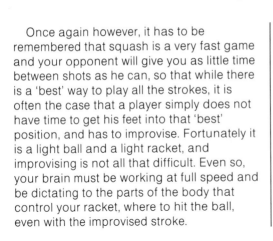

Once again however, it has to be remembered that squash is a very fast game and your opponent will give you as little time between shots as he can, so that while there is a 'best' way to play all the strokes, it is often the case that a player simply does not have time to get his feet into that 'best' position, and has to improvise. Fortunately it is a light ball and a light racket, and improvising is not all that difficult. Even so, your brain must be working at full speed and be dictating to the parts of the body that control your racket, where to hit the ball, even with the improvised stroke.

*Moving in for the backhand drive.*

*Transfer your weight on to the leading foot.*

## The back corners

Now for the back corners. If the ball is well and truly in the corner, it will not be possible to return it except by 'boasting' it up on to the side wall. This has to be an upward shot and not a particularly hard one. An upward flick is much more likely to carry on to the front wall than a tremendous 'blast' at the ball. You should play the shot facing the rear wall, or even as far round as facing the other side wall, and then play as though to drive the ball against the side wall. At the last moment use your wrist to flick the ball upwards and as far forward as possible on to that wall, whence it should carry to the opposite front corner. If this has been achieved, it is now vital to get out of the corner as fast as possible and try to cover the various shots possible for your opponent from the weak shot you have been forced to play from his previous good length shot.

## Using your brain!

However, whilst obviously the body and racket play a vital part, so does your brain. You must turn that into a squash computer as soon as you can. You must learn by

*Follow through upwards.*

experience to feed all the relevant information into it concerning the court (height, temperature, floor, and any peculiarities), the ball (fast or slow), the opponent (old, young, experienced or not, favourite shots, weaknesses, etc.) and any other information, such as your own fitness (I'm exhausted, must go for quick winners, etc.), the event (if I win this, I play the next round this evening, so must not get exhausted now) and so on. The aim is that the computer should then give an accurate 'read out' as you approach the ball, and tell you every time what is likely to be the most effective shot. It takes time to train your computer and to learn to feed all the right information into it, but is well worth the effort.

*Above: The correct position for retrieving the ball in the back corner. Note that the body is well clear of both the side and back walls and facing the opposite side of the court. The aim here is to get under the ball and hit it hard, high and as far forward on the side wall as possible.*

*Top left: The wrong position from which to retrieve the ball from the rear corner.*

*Top right: Moving into the right position, well clear of the side wall.*

*Bottom left: Make a full swing, clear of the back wall, with the racket well under the ball.*

*Bottom right: Follow through upwards, the eyes following the ball and the feet still in position.*

# THE · SERVICE

Bearing in mind what we have just said about the desirability of putting your opponent under pressure in the back corners, it is obviously sensible to develop a service which does just that, and will hopefully lead to an advantageous position in a rally which will give you a point, if you win it. The service is the one shot which you can play from the precise position you choose, and not when running to a ball hit by your opponent. It is therefore possible to take up the best position in your own time.

There is very little likelihood of playing an outright winner, an ace, in squash. In tennis a player hits the ball as hard as he can, either wide of his opponent or down the centre line, and not infrequently blasts it past him. It is very different in squash; a very hard hit service will be slowed up by the front wall, and even if it passes your opponent, will rebound far enough from the rear wall to make it easy for him to retrieve. So there is no percentage in the hard hit service.

The most likely service to cause problems is the high lob, but it needs to be played very accurately. Mathematicians will appreciate the use of 'angles' – if the server strikes the ball from as far forward and as close to the side wall as possible with his rear foot correctly grounded within the service box, he can then play a wider angle on the front wall, so that the ball will then make a more direct (i.e. less of a glancing blow) contact with the opposite side wall.

The more direct the contact, the more pace it takes off it. The ball should then drop on to the floor before hitting the back wall; this will slow it up even more, so that if the receiver allows it to reach the back wall, it will hardly rebound far enough for him to get it back. The aim then is to hit the ball

**Jahangir Khan and Tristan Nancarrow: Jahangir attempts a forehand drop from the T.**

upwards towards the front wall, so that it will hit it approximately in the centre of the top panel, between the cut and out of court lines. It will then carry on upwards, and hopefully strike the side wall just below the out of court line about halfway between the opposite service box and the back wall, dropping to the floor in the corner. This should force the receiver to play a very difficult shot at the ball between its contacts with the side and rear walls.

In cricket one is always exhorted to 'play straight', the theory being that if the ball is approaching along a certain line and the bat is moving up that line in the opposite direction, it is bound to make contact. The cricket coach then explains all the disasters that will befall if you hit across the line of the ball.

This is precisely what the good lob service forces the retriever to do in squash. He has to try to hit across the ball in two directions – firstly the ball is dropping fast and secondly it is coming off the wall. Obviously this increases his chances of a mis-hit, and even if he eliminates one of the risks, by hitting the ball straight back towards the side wall, it can only mean that the ball will then go to the opposite front corner for an easy shot for the server, who ought to be able to play a winner. So much for the advantages of the lob service: they are well worth the practice you will need to perfect it.

But there are also risks, however, due to the fact that the ball has to travel high over the centre of the court area and hit the side wall as close to the out of court line as possible. This means that there is a danger of hitting the ball out and losing the service. The danger is of course increased in courts with low ceilings or beams, dangling lights and the like, or with a very fast and volatile ball. In the case of the latter, you also have to consider the fact that even if the server takes the risk of hitting a lob service out, and achieves the service he is hoping for, the chance of it being a winner or gaining an advantage are much reduced by the very

# THE · FOREHAND · SERVICE

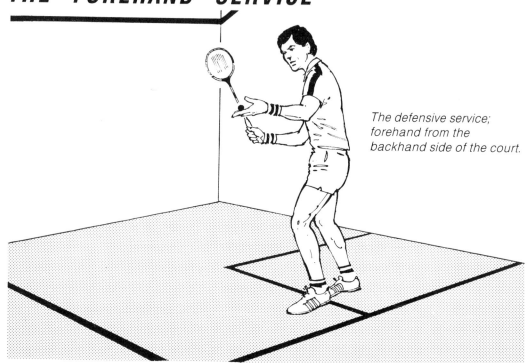

The defensive service; forehand from the backhand side of the court.

A good throw up is all important.

# TECHNIQUE

Strike the ball well over towards the centre of the court.

Follow through fully, and then you will need only one step to be in position on the T.

'bounciness' of the ball. Quite simply this means that it is more likely to rebound into an open space from which the receiver will be more likely to have a fairly unhampered go at it.

## Putting pressure on your opponent

There will therefore be occasions, depending on the ball and the court, when even a normally accurate lob server may decide that the risk is just not worthwhile, and he will look for an alternative. There is no other type of service so likely to produce a winner, so the aim now must be to prevent any kind of aggressive return by the receiver.

This brings us back to the same point about putting pressure on your opponent by forcing him to play the ball close to one, or preferably two, walls. The lob services must always be hit on the forehand from the forehand side of the court, and the backhand from the other side. This is the only way the ball can be struck close to the side wall to achieve the widest angle on the front wall.

The situation is completely different in the case of the defensive service. The aim now is to narrow the angle on the front wall by striking the ball as far across court as possible towards the T area with the rear foot still inside the service box. The ball is then 'driven' just above the cut line, using a backhand stroke from the forehand side and vice versa. The ball should hit the side wall a few feet behind the opposite service box to as good a length as possible. To narrow the angle as far as possible, it also helps to strike the ball from the rear of the service box.

In these ways, the shot can be made to keep close to the side wall, and hopefully finish up in the corner. The receiver ought to be able to return it, but his options will be strictly limited. It is also possible with this service to observe any change of position by the receiver, as one is now facing across court, and can adjust the service.

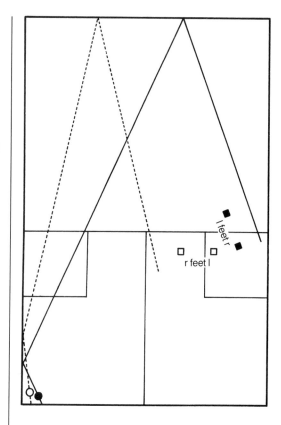

■ *feet positions for lob service.*
□ *feet positions for defensive service.*
● *where the lob service should land.*
○ *where the defensive service should land.*

It is a real pity that many good players do not make more use of the opportunities offered by a good service. They simply get the ball into play again somehow, often hitting the service as they stroll into the service box. It is difficult enough to score points in squash and it seems very stupid to throw away what should be a definite advantage. Try hard to make every service count – it will help your game!

**Correct preparation for a backhand by Susan Devoy of New Zealand.**

# RETURNING · THE · SERVICE

After the service, the return of service should be the second easiest shot in squash. The server has to hit it into a very limited area, within which the receiver can take up whatever position he thinks best, sure that the ball is bound to come within reach. I usually advise a beginner to stand close to the centre court rear corner of the service area and to watch the ball from the moment it is struck. He should then move forward and towards the side wall in order to take the ball at a convenient spot well clear of the walls.

However well the server hits it, he cannot make the ball cling to the side wall and then turn at a right angle along the back wall, It must at some stage pass through a 3D triangle, about a foot and a half from the two walls. This may be on its way towards the corner, or as it comes off the side wall, but every service must give the receiver his chance to play it 'in the clear', and experience will tell him where that clear area is going to be as the service approaches. It is always better to stand at the back of the court and move forward to the ball, than

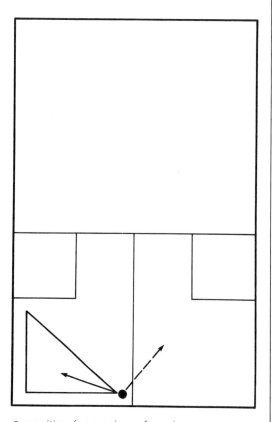

● position for receiver of service.
→ movement forward and sideways into the triangle.
— — → eyes watching server.

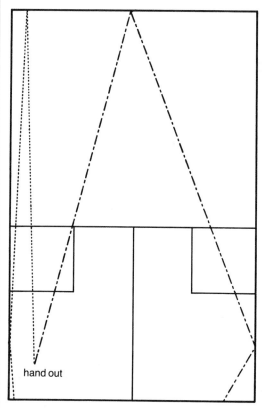

hand out

Two useful service returns: the drive down the nearest side wall, and the cross court lob over the 'oaktree'.

stand too far up towards the service box area and find that you are having to move backwards for a good lob, not sure when you are going to run into the back wall.

The main points to remember for the return of service are the same as for any shot in the rally now starting: (a) play a shot which will not return to the T area where your opponent will have planted his oaktree, and (b), either hit the ball into one of the other three quarters of the court, so that you can move directly to the T without fear of causing a collision, or if you hit it back into the same quarter, then be prepared to move sideways fast out of the 'slice of cake' and then up to the T.

The safest and most normal returns are either down the nearest side wall (either a drive or a lob) to as good a length as possible, or high across court, over the 'oaktree' into the opposite back corner. The

*Return of service – the correct position for the beginner. Stand close to the back wall to judge the length of the ball, keeping eyes on the server to gain maximum anticipation time, and ready to move forward into the 'triangle' to intercept the good service at a convenient spot.*

aim of both these shots is to impose the usual two-wall pressure. Of course, on good days or against an opponent who has shown himself vulnerable to certain forms of attack, it is perfectly possible to vary your returns and include the occasional drop shot or angle, if the service gives you room for something a little more ambitious. For example, drop shots will be very effective against a slow-moving opponent, who has shown a marked reluctance to move quickly towards the front of the court.

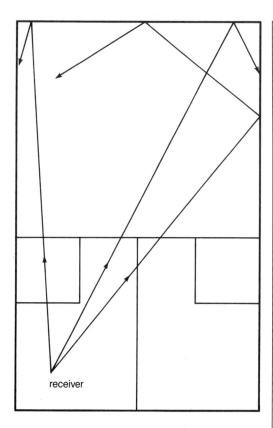

*Three attacking returns of service – the straight and cross court drop volleys and the reverse angle. The same shots can be played, even if the ball has bounced, as ground strokes.*

# THE · RALLY

Once the rally is launched, both players will seek to gain the initiative, move as economically and quickly as possible to and from the T, make the opponent move further and eventually manoeuvre him out of position so that the ball can be hit where he cannot possibly get to it. Basically the aim is to keep him in the rear corners of the court, hoping that sooner or later the ball will be so awkward that he will be forced to boast it out

and set up the chance for a winner from an easy position in the front of the court.

In a long match, however, stamina becomes a major factor, and it is obviously more tiring for your opponent if he has to move further at each exchange of shots. Thus, if you hit the ball three feet from the side wall, you can then, by a more accurate shot than his, force him to play his next shot only one foot from the wall and he will have to move further from the T to get to it. Although only a short distance, if this is kept up for long periods, it becomes very significant.

Another point to bear in mind is variety of

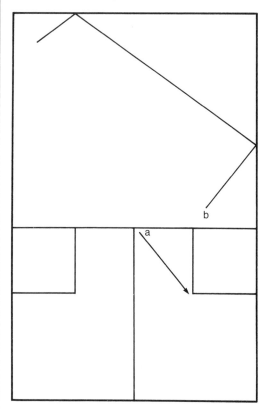

*A is assuming that B is going to drive down the right-hand wall. B, however, instead plays an attacking angle to the opposite corner.*

*The forehand reverse angle. Note that the feet are in the normal position and that there is nothing to allow the opponent to anticipate the direction of the shot. This is a particularly useful shot on a fast court, where an angle 'sliding' across the front wall will draw the opponent further up the court than a drop shot which rebounds a long way.*

shot. This has a number of facets. Firstly, if you can make your opponent assume that a certain shot is probable, he may well start moving to where he thinks the ball is going, and may then find it difficult to 'alter course' if you vary the shot and hit the ball somewhere completely different.

Secondly, it may well be that under certain conditions with a particular ball, some shots will be less rewarding than on other occasions. For example, on a very hot court with an inevitably hot and high bouncing ball, the normal drop shot is not likely to be successful. In the first place it will be difficult to control and play accurately, and even if you do play it well, it will come leaping back down the court again and be easy for your opponent to get to. All the risk will result in little chance of a winner.

In these conditions, it is still important to get your opponent moving up and down the court, and the only way to get the ball to stay in the front of the court is by sliding it across the face of the front wall by an angle or reverse angle, rather than by a drop which hits the wall direct.

On the question of wrongfooting your opponent, once again it is the angle or reverse angle that supplies the variety. The three most common instances of this are: firstly, when you have been making repeated use of the drive down the nearest side wall, Again you shape up as if to play this and your opponent starts moving to the appropriate back corner. However you now hit the ball on to the side wall instead, so that it rebounds to the opposite front corner.

Secondly, if you have been driving the ball across court fairly regularly, just as your opponent anticipates another, and starts moving for it, you can wrongfoot him by the reverse angle, again into the unexpected, diametrically opposite front corner.

Thirdly, if you have been consistently playing drops, you can very often fool your opponent, who is now anticipating another drop and approaching on the wall side of

the striker, by playing an angle which takes the ball to the other side of the court.

There are three ways of playing an angle shot. One is by moving the position of your feet in order to play a normal shot, but now at the side wall rather than the front. This is the least efficient way of playing angles as it gives clear advance notice of what your intention is to your opponent. The second is to hit the ball very early for a reverse angle, and pull it across your body to the far wall, or very late for a normal angle and hit at the near wall. Again, an alert opponent will be able to read this, and by far the best way of playing angles is to hit the ball at the normal time but with a racket angled by your wrist to hit the ball at a side wall. With practice you will soon master this essential stroke.

*The correct approach to a ball in the front forehand corner. Any of the eight possible shots may be played.*

## Stroke production

This brings us to discuss normal stroke production. A correct squash shot is a similar action to 'whipping'. The racket is taken back with a 'cocked wrist' and then whipped through so that your arm and racket are more or less parallel with the floor, and the power taken off by an upward follow through. The long full-arm tennis back swing – necessary with the heavy ball and racket – has no place in squash. Not only is it not necessary with the light ball and racket, but it is dangerous with your opponent nearby and can also lead to problems if the ball does something unexpected. There is not time to get the racket to the ball if it has been extended behind you, whereas a quick wrist flick would get the ball up.

The upward follow through should follow the line of the boards on the floor on which you are standing, and not – especially on the backhand – follow round and across court, where it may well hit or obstruct your opponent. If your arm and racket are parallel to the floor at the moment of contact, the wrist can then be used to produce an angle shot which would not be possible if they were in a vertical position.

# *PREPARATIONS*

I have already stressed the need to be in good physical shape before venturing on to a squash court. There are, though, obviously ways of sharpening that normal good health into the peak necessary for improved play. Here, I think, we have to differentiate between the full-time player, who is making his living, or part of it, out of the game, and the ordinary club player, who has a normal job and the usual family commitments. It is a simple difference of time availability. The vast majority of club players have a very limited time at their disposal, and cannot afford to spend hours in the gymnasium or doing weight training and circuits. Furthermore, such luxuries are very expensive.

*Note the flexibility of the wrist in this backhand shot. The ball can easily be flicked over to the forehand side.*

# SQUASH

Another point is that squash is all about hitting a squash ball with a squash racket against a squash court wall. All the running in the world will be of no avail if you cannot hit the ball accurately. Extreme fitness is of very little use if you do not have the skill to prolong the match to the point where your extra fitness can begin to give you the advantage. There is little point in coming off court convinced that you could have outlasted your opponent, if only he had not won, by superior racket skill, and by three games to love, before you could prove your point! I therefore strongly advise those of you who have only a limited amount of spare time to spend on practice to spend that time on court.

It is not only your legs, lungs and muscles that have to be at their most effective, it is your brain and your ability to use your racket well. Every time you approach the ball when it is your turn to play it, your brain must give a positive instruction to the rest of the body as to what shot is most in your interest. It is not enough just to go up to the ball and give it a whack in the general direction of the front wall. The 'inner computer' must have balanced up a large number of factors and come up with the right solution.

Such factors are things like – 'my opponent is weaker on the backhand than the forehand; he is slow to change direction; last time I played the ball from this position I played a drop, so perhaps I had better do something different; I must be careful about lobbing on this court with that low beam; my angles are not working too well today, so I had better cut them out for a while; I am feeling very fit and he is looking a bit worse for wear, so all in all, I think I had better go for a drive down the side wall.' Your brain will only get the necessary practice in thinking along these lines if it is taken on to a court as frequently as possible and given the opportunity to improve.

Allied to this is the ability to produce correctly the shots ordered by the 'computer'. There is little point in the computer coming up with the correct choice of shot, after bearing in mind all the relevant pros and cons, if the playing mechanism cannot produce the goods. Again, jogging round the block several hundred times will not help the brain to work or the stroke production. This can only be improved on court, so any spare time you have, spend it on court if at all possible.

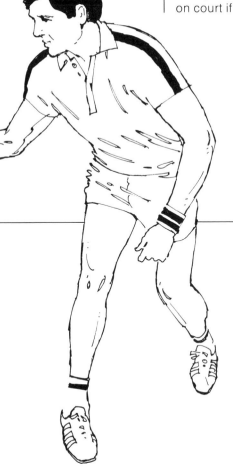

*Left: Correct preparation for the backhand. Note how the eyes are fixed firmly on the ball as it approaches. Middle: The ball is struck level with the front foot, and the weight is transferred to the front foot as the shot is played.*
*Right: Correct follow through on the backhand. The racket is being taken away upwards, and not round the body where it might endanger the opponent.*

# *PRACTICE*

Fortunately, squash is not only a tremendously enjoyable game to play but it can also be made a thoroughly enjoyable game at which to practise. The rules dictate how a match must be played, but of course you and a friend can make up your own rules if you decide that you want to practise some aspect of the game.

For example, you both want to improve your fitness but do not want to spend your evenings jogging. You may therefore decide to play an otherwise normal game with all the normal rules except that you allow each other to return the ball on the second or third bounce, rather than the first, and this will obviously prolong the rallies very considerably and will provide fitness training plus the chance to improve stroke production and get the 'computer' working.

Players vary considerably in their attitudes to practice. Some are able to go on to a court on their own and practise particular shots for hours. Others get bored very quickly with just hitting the ball back to themselves, and want the competitive element of another player, even if they are then going to adapt the rules rather than play a proper game. Those who can practise on their own can often achieve great accuracy with certain shots, but the weakness of this sort of practice is that you are always aware of where the ball is coming from, and at what speed, because you hit the previous shot. In a match, or even a practice game, however, the other player has hit the previous shot and you will not be able to. forecast quite as precisely exactly when and where you are going to be able to hit it.

My advice then is to arrange practice with a friend whenever possible, and help each other as much as possible. You may have to take it in turns to act as the 'fall guy' for each other. For example, you may want to practise lobs, while he wants to concentrate on his angles. For the first ten minutes or so, you will be playing your lobs while he retrieves

them from the rear corners and you continue lobbing. Then it will be your turn to stand near the front wall on the backhand side of the court 'feeding' the ball to positions between him and the forehand wall so that he can play his forehand angles.

Let me suggest a few tried and proven ways for two players to practise together for their mutual benefit. Before that however, I would suggest that you play as nearly as possible to normal match rules and so make it as near the real thing as you can – rather like using live bullets in the final army training for genuine battle conditions. Secondly, these practice games do not demand that the two players are of similar ability. Finally, squash is a highly competitive game with all the pressures and tensions that winning and losing create. In most cases, it is possible and desirable to introduce some method of scoring, thereby introducing this element as well into the practice.

## Varieties of practice games

The first sort of game I would like to suggest is where one player agrees to lob from the front of the court, while his opponent – whether forced to by the accuracy of the lob or not – will boast the ball out of the corner, and so set up the next lob from the opposite front quarter of the court. Once this has been working satisfactorily for a while, varieties can be introduced.

For this practice to be of genuine use, however, each player must return to the T between each shot, and this of course applies when the variations are used as well. After all, in a proper match – and that is what you are practising for – you are not going to be allowed to stand in one corner of the court, certain that the ball is going to be hit back to you. Also, it is not only the actual playing of the shot that is important, it is the movement towards the ball, getting into position and then playing the shot that matters, and that you can only practise if you make it necessary to come from the T each time. It is also good training for getting back to the T before your opponent can play his next shot, so that although you know in a practice situation what that next shot is going to be, you will not know in a match, and need to be on the T to cover all the possibilities open to him.

The first variation is when the player in the front of the court decides to shift from lobs across court to drives or lobs down the side wall. The player in the back of the court continues to boast, so the 'rallies' now continue up and down each side wall in turn. A useful variation, which must not be overdone or it will ruin the main aim of the practice, is for each occasionally to test whether the other chap is genuinely returning to the T between shots as he should be.

For example, the player in the front can occasionally play a drop shot instead of the lob. If his opponent is correctly on the T he ought to be able to get to the ball, or somewhere near it, whereas if he has not bothered to get to the T, this will be apparent. Similarly, the player in the rear of the court can occasionally, when the inaccuracy of a lob permits, play the ball straight down the wall to the corner from which he has hit it. If the lobber has been idle and stayed in the front of the court, he will not get near it, but if he has come back to the T he will.

It is important to remember in this sort of practice to change roles every so often, so that both participants get the full benefit. Obviously this practice can be extended so that eventually the player in the front of the court is allowed to play any lob or drive, down the wall or across court, and the player in the back can play any angle or drop to the front of the court that the length of his opponent's shot permits.

The second suggestion is a game that takes place in the front of the court only. It is in its own right a lot of fun and very enjoyable. Both players are restricted to playing only angles and reverse angles – in other words every shot must hit one of the side walls before it hits the front wall. To many squash players, especially those who have come to squash from games like tennis or badminton where there are no walls, it would seem that they regard the walls purely as things to keep the roof up. They are in fact the things that give squash its wide variety of shots, and probably produce more opportunities for wrongfooting opponents than anything else. This little game forces the players to 'think angles', it makes the players' actual stroke production of the angles that much better, and it gives each player a repeated view of his opponent playing these shots, and this can only improve his anticipation of an opponent

about to play an angle in his next proper match. It also gives both players valuable experience at keeping out of each other's way in a more than usually limited area.

Another useful way of practising for two players whose standards are not too different is to play a normal match, but in the first game, player A plays purely defensively, while B can produce whatever shots he chooses in his efforts to play winners. One has to accept that defensive play has a major role in a squash match; only too often, you find your opponent is leading 6-3 for example. At that moment, it is vital that he does not score again and so it is necessary to make it as difficult for him to do so as possible. It is essential to cut out any ambitious shots like drops from the back of the court or reverse angles, where the risk of failure and of presenting him with a point are too high, and instead concentrate on pinning him in the rear corners, hoping that he will eventually fail to get the ball up, or will set up an easy winner in the front.

Of course if you are the player who is leading 6-3, you will be eager to win those final points that will give you the game, and it is good practice for you to try and manufacture winners against the purely defensive tactics of your opponent. Both players can therefore get much useful match practice from this, provided they again remember that after each game, they change roles so that both get the maximum benefit.

**Lucy Soutter prepares for a forehand drive.**

# USEFUL
# ADDRESSES

**Squash Rackets Association**
Francis House
Francis Street
London SW1P 1DE
01-828-3064/6

**Women's Squash Rackets Association**
345 Upper Richmond Road West
Sheen
London
SW14 8QN
01-876-6219

**International Squash Rackets Federation**
93 Cathedral Road
Cardiff
Wales
CF1 9TG
0222-374771

**Women's International Squash Rackets Federation**
93 Cathedral Road
Cardiff
Wales
CF1 9TG
0222-374771

**United States Squash Rackets Association**
211 Ford Road
Bala-Cynwyd
Pennsylvania
PA19004
USA
0101-215-667-4006

# RULES CLINIC

# INDEX

# INDEX